Duties of the Spirit

for Claire,
It's so nice to be
getting to you & to
look forward to knowing
you better   warmly
Pat Fargnoli

Duties of the Spirit

Patricia Fargnoli

Patricia Fargnoli

TUPELO PRESS

Duties of the Spirit
Copyright © 2005 Patricia Fargnoli
ISBN 1-932195-21-1
ISBN-13: 978-1-932195-21-7
Printed in USA

First paperback edition April 2005
Library of Congress Control Number 2004114633
Tupelo Press
PO Box 539, Dorset, Vermont 05251
802.366.8185 · Fax 802.362.1883
editor@tupelopress.org · web www.tupelopress.org

Cover painting: "Last Light" Edythe T. Donovan
Cover and text designed by William Kuch, WK Graphic Design

For my grandchildren: Alycia, Joe, Joshua—
those lights

Contents

one/

two/

three/

one/

The Invitation

I have opened the doors
near the garden.
Why don't you come into
the unfolding
of Japanese fans?
The peacocks are strolling
among the lobelia
for no one but you
in this place where
the impossible
is shaking
its bright turquoise feathers.
I have turned
off the radio,
washed purple and green grapes
for the pedestal table,
filled frosted goblets
with fresh well water.
Afterwards the bed,
its turned down silk.
What you have left behind
will forget you
soon enough.

First Night at The Frost Place

The bat veered erratically over us
on that first nervous night,
while we ate, the twelve of us, at long tables
in the three-sided shed behind the lodge
protected from the summer rain—
which was hammering straight down—
and the lightning.

A thing so dark, it seemed
snipped from the burlap of shadow
high in the rafters above our candlelight.
Something not real—a figment,
a frantic silhouette.
And all the while we
(who were not terribly disturbed)

continued to pass the good food,
continued to reach tentatively,
stranger to stranger. Oh
we were jovial—we told jokes,
we laughed, we cracked open the closed
doors of ourselves to each other.

And, for all that society, I
might have missed it entirely—
so far above us it fluttered.
Seen/unseen. Seen/unseen.

Talking to Myself in This Late Year

New Harbor, Maine

Already, the wings of strange birds are starting up
from the crosshatched mats of marsh grasses.
Greetings, little strangers, and goodbye.

The sky is white as northern glaciers
or sheets in a bleach-filled washer—
or it is nothing, an absence.

Last night I dreamed I was hunting for protection,
a safe house hidden on a city street. Blood on its door.

There is no danger in the way the heart guards itself
from the sweet darkness

or there is danger in the way the heart guards itself

or the darkness is never sweet.

Even in the second week of September, the sea
enamels itself with a brilliance that comes
from the start of cold weather.

Where did youth go?
Not to mention marriage and motherhood.

Three white schooners ride the tide,
even while anchored in the radiating sunlight.

And two American huskies
are tethered for a walk, white fur long
like the thick and delicate fibers of a Greek carpet.

Yes, I am getting old;
yes, being poor takes too much out of me.

Here is the safe way station, filled with the seaweed
scent of salt. The waves emit light
as if from a thousand windows.

Happiness

The old couple sit on the stone ledge to their stucco house,
laughing, while the bells ring in the village.

There are stones embedded in the earth, and scant grass.
The wall of the house behind them is very old,
storm-stained, time-stained.

The sheep wander into the dooryard and eat the grass.
Did I say the house is very old? Yes,

and the stones embedded in the earth and the sheep
are old and the flowered house dress of the woman,
the dusty shoes of the man, the teeth the man is missing—all old.

This must be Italy, or maybe France. I'll never know.
But I know about age and laughter—even about missing teeth.

The woman's arm, which is wrinkled like linen, touches the man's.
Or his arm touches hers—it's hard to tell. She wears no ring.

And the man has one of those flat wool caps the Irish wear.
Maybe they are Irish and have lived through The Troubles.
Maybe they remember hunger.

And because they are old, I know people have died in their lives.
Friends with hearts that burned out, sons caught
in a crossfire—something like that.

There is history in this story. And the couple is embedded in it.
They know this, but they don't think about it.
The sheep don't know it, nor the grass.

Theirs is a young history, since we call
wherever they are "the old country,"
and the couple is probably dead by now.

.

I'll bet they buried him in his absence of teeth
with his black horn-rimmed glasses,

and her next to him under a matching stone
in her scrubbed-thin dress, her blue socks, her sandals.
Bet they kept her watch on.

In Sorrento, widows come with buckets of water
and scrub brushes to wash the graves.
In another country, the villagers walk to the cemetery
after the evening meal to bring the ancestors
news of the day's catch.

I'd like to do something like that for these two.
I'd bring them bread. I'd ask them

do you remember the day of the photograph
or why you were happy?

I doubt they'd know it—
happiness arrives for one moment
and then flees past the sheep, down the lane,

toward the village where the bells
are always ringing for someone.

Walking on Reservoir Road

To walk is to go forward into the landscape where trees billow
under the wind like waves, you moving beneath their ocean,

to go where cows lay their acquiescent bodies down in ochre
and timothy denying the myth that rain will come soon,

to pour your strength into your heels and out onto Reservoir Road
or any road, to move breath through your core and lung's wings,

release it through half-opened lips into the welcoming air,
to take in the chill and moisture and tannic smell of the brook

as it pours over heaped cold bottomstones, the flat, round,
angular, shining blue/brown/gray stones,

is to press yourself to the world until you become one
with its thrusting body. It is to, yes, go forward past white berries

studding the bare bush branches, the white-faced hornet hive
hung low from a thin maple limb like a paper lantern,

green algae's velvet-thick blanket on the pasture pond,
while across the valley, shadows lay wide black wings across

blurred blue mountains, and forward as the everywhere bell-burble
of downfalling runnels and ripples spills through the woods.

It is to pass by each white house with its barn, each well,
each stack of old baskets, the six brown horses on the hill—

to leave all behind, to let those two chocolate labs, who dash
from the last farmhouse barking, run on ahead of you, lead you

forward into leaf mold's musty perfume, into the unknowing
and unknown of the next half mile, to trust faith and the strength

of your own two fine thighs, to push yourself beyond where
even the dogs turn back at their master's homing call.

Evidence

When I walked in the forest it was April.
Deer pellets were mounded here and there
on fallen leaves and under low cedar branches.

Twice I saw scat—I couldn't tell what it signified.
When I stopped to listen, the wild was silent
except for the rumble of the logging truck far away.

The duff was spongy beneath my sneakers.
I walked carefully, and as far in as I dared,
trying to keep sight of the road and the field.

But the forest drew me into its vast density.
I lost the road, the field, and all sense of direction.
Once I bent to touch two waxy fingers

reaching up from the forest floor,
and once to run both palms over a stump
wholly green and soft with moss.

Near a marshy place, a wagon wheel leaned
against a hillock. It had been there so long
it was the antique green/brown of a Roman relic.

It began to rain.
Once I heard hooves snapping fallen branches.
They were always behind me.

I turned in a full circle; and turned again,
I saw nothing
but I swear I heard some spirit go away
brushing its sharp antlers against the trees.

The Undeniable Pressure of Existence

I saw the fox running by the side of the road
past the turned-away brick faces of the condominiums
past the Citco gas station with its line of cars and trucks
and he ran, limping, gaunt, matted dull haired
past Jim's Pizza, past the Wash-O-Mat
past the Thai Garden, his sides heaving like bellows
and he kept running to where the interstate
crossed the state road and he reached it and ran on
under the underpass and beyond it past the perfect
rows of split-levels, their identical driveways
their brookless and forestless yards,
and from my moving car, I watched him,
helpless to do anything to help him, certain he was beyond
any aid, any desire to save him, and he ran loping on,
far out of his element, sick, panting, starving,
his eyes fixed on some point ahead of him,
some possible salvation
in all this hopelessness, that only he could see.

If Too Much Has Happened

Even the rain speaks in syllables
that can't be found in our language
and so do the crows
                              loud on the high slim branches
as if testing the sky,
and so do the stones that fall down
the shale cliffs, rattling their hard tongues.
                    Have you ever noticed
how empty spaces are filled with thought,
the way, for example, everything
that has ever happened in a house
fills the rooms of that house?

In my old house on Deerfield Road,
the outline of a French Revolutionary captain
could be seen in the cracks of my bedroom ceiling
and beside him, a child—
                    no older than I was—
also held there in the plaster,
for who knows how long—
her hair falling around her shoulders.

                    I'd lie awake for hours
through the long summer twilights,
imagining their lives in that house,
so long before mine, and telling them
the sadness for which I had no words—
                    and no other listeners.

Who could say they didn't answer?
Their response in the tambourine of rain
on the tin porch roof beyond my window,
or in the code of car lights moving across the walls.
                    When my parents died,
the aunts pretended nothing had happened.
What could not be spoken
was held in the muscles and flesh of my body.

And you, too, have your sorrow
that can find no expression.
                    What cannot be expressed hangs
thinner than dust and as ubiquitous,
in the shafts of sun that travel silently
                    and from a great distance.

Fun

Of course when I think about fun,
I think of a man in a short buckskin skirt,
shirtless, walking down the street
of the Bridge of Flowers,
with a crossbow, a quiver of arrows on his back.
About fifty, an ordinary man
I wouldn't have noticed
but for the crossbow and his half-nakedness—
in other words, his way of sticking out
in the crowd of tourists going by.
He was just walking, a man in a suit
walking beside him, both of them
with a sense of purpose,
both obviously on the way to somewhere.
The street slanted up a little and they bent forward
to accommodate it. That must have been
their mission that day—onward and upward.
The bow rattled on his back,
the arrows quivered.
His hair was white—if that helps.
The problem with such fun
is that nobody explains it. It enters stage-left
and goes off stage-right into the wings.
Then for years it keeps going off in your mind
like flashbulbs. It takes on weight, metaphor:
Father Death, Creative Spirit.
Gosh I wish I'd known the whole story—
I could put the puzzle to bed then—
if only I knew the meaning of it all.

From a Clifftop Overlooking Pigeon Island

The Guadeloupe day stalls and refuses to advance
                                        among the coral reefs.
A blessing, this hammock.
North and South swaying between the two palms. Slight wind.

I offer up this peace without knowing where it goes
                and fold the woven cloth over me, a cocoon from rain
                                        which has just begun.
Protected, I am rocking—in the sweet odor of the rain.

Here is the poem in aqua, and the colorful fish
darting over the shoals, erasing the tideline and remaking it.

I am done with trying to do something significant with my life.
The only need I have is this enclosure, this day
                                folding around me,
and beyond the cliff, the sea alive with silver.

Quotidian Poem

When I heard the bombing
had begun I drove down
to Keene and bought
a 3x magnifying glass,
a sketch book
and drawing pencils. Then,
I went out behind the apartments
to snap off seed pods, weeds
I could not name
and a couple of brittle leaves.
I saved the afternoon
by studying edges
of petals, seeds,
the marvelous veins,
by sketching them.
On the page, I wrote:
unknown weeds 10/7/01, found
on the day we began bombing
in the patch between Applewood
and the Historical Museum.
Then, I made a pot of soup
out of black-eyed peas
and a ham bone
I'd frozen from Easter.
I threw in onions, garlic,
parsley, cumin,
a couple of tomatoes—
whatever made sense.
Enough for an army.

The Last Day

Let's say it begins at six o'clock
on April's first morning when the sun has risen
to vibrate three inches above the mountain
and light shimmies along three wires looped
from the tall trunk of the pine to the house
where you are not awake yet,
though a few birds sail the lower air
near the just-thawed ground. Boughs still
heavy with cones lie scattered, and beyond the stolid
granite church with its black windows,
one bird sings the sweetest notes into being.
Stalks are rising—exploding in yellow
in last year's garden and one ladybug climbs
the screen—as if it had all the time in the world.

The Village

A little after noon. The village carillon
plays something in a minor key.
Bell notes bounce against the winter sky—
solid blue after days washed with gray.
A woodpecker raps against the highest trunk,
and what melted in yesterday's rain
has frozen into sheets of ice.
Walking's treacherous.
February smells of iron.
Main Street's visible through the trees.
At the post office cars shuttle
townsfolk in and out—
mail-gatherers at the boxes.
The country's on high alert again.
Here is the life I know:
crow each morning on the same
furred branch,
Walpole Historical Society Museum,
white and churchlike on the hill,
a town so picture-perfect
it's been laid out
in a coffee table book.
Above me, in the giant maple,
one branch lies winter-snapped
and ready to fall but for the way
it's cradled across two other limbs.
One good wind would bring it down.

Bach: The Goldberg Variations;
Aria and Thirty Variations; Glen Gould, Pianist

Now gray light
    and shadow move over the surface,
a slow boat motors out this music flying to it
        across the lake.
The husk of an insect (a dragonfly?) flutters
    from the porch screen of the cottage,

carcass blown thin and grave,
 wings still perfect
  in their trawling net design.

The porch has twelve windows,
       two doors
and the pewter light of the lake easily enters it.

The pianist's fingers move with deliberation
as they create the world
    and leave off to silence.

Then a thunder of hands   a burst
of notes drumming gypsies whirling.

Then a necklace   beads rolling
    from the broken string.

On the water
  shadow wings alternate
    with bars of light.

Someone knocks at the next house.
  The net of life is going on.

Gould's fingers hurry across the keys   then slow
              like the beginning of rain.

two/

Answers for the Scientists Who Have Wired the Heads of Zebra Finches to Study Their Dreams

They dream in song, of course, birds do: hundred songs
of the marsh wren, twenty of song sparrow, three hundred calls
of the crow, each bird naming itself in melody or hoot, rasp,

whistle, squawk, drumming. Such a Babel. No,
a concerto. Interval and time signature, staccato,
legato, tremolo, the retardando of evening.

They dream sounds we cannot hear,
things we cannot see or feel—
infrasounds, ultraviolet light, magnetic fields of the earth.

They dream the north and west of flowers, longitude
and latitude of home. This is what they sing
in their wide-eyed sleep: blueprints for the nest,

twigs woven in careful design, spider silk,
lump of cow dung, clay, all made strange by sleep's narcotic.
They dream dive down and scatter up, drift on thermal,

balance on bough, bank and turn. They dream the currents
of flyway, wind pattern, star pattern; they give new names
to the constellations—bug names, flower names.

With their faster hearts, faster lives
they sing ten notes to the one note we hear;
they dream also ten dreams to our one.

Ten times the dreamwork to undo the stress of storm,
sickness, attack of snake on the nest. Ten times
the beak-language and solos that rise

out of sub-song into fullness. With what intelligence,
what emotion (how can you not believe this!)
do they dream of us with our gangly bodies, our instruments

and books, our feeding tables and earnest eyes?
Or do they dream of us at all;
are we to them of such small consequence?

The Small Hurtling Bodies

attracted by the light, sometimes small birds would fly
at the lighthouses smashing through the glass

Perhaps it was storm that left them dazed,
unable to measure direction, confusing up and down,
ground and sky, or perhaps it was the brightness
that promised some sort of relief from the raging night.
Or was it simply that there was no choice
so that without thought, without even time
for thought, they hurled themselves
toward the light, their wings, their bright bodies flung
through glass, flung at the beacon meant as warning,
flung at the source itself until feathers and smashed glass
sprayed out north, east, south, west.
And the debris fell with a sound like crushing ice,
no, louder, much louder, and it showered down,
littered floor, stairs, the ground, all the reachable spaces,
so that whoever was near that place at the time
was covered with glass, was pummeled, transformed,
torn open by the small hurtling bodies.

Poem for a Composer at Eighty-Three

for Juli Nunlist

So we go into the old
                    house where Juli lives
to hear her compositions

of Rilke's poems, a cycle:
                    Du gehst mit, Lied vom Meer,

You Come Too, Song from the Sea,
                    and the others, sung
on tape by the soprano

who gets them exactly right—
                    each note expressing grief, and

longing, along with beauty—
                    without which, the best
music, like the world, would be

nothing. So silent we keep—
                    in the small, beamed, wainscotted

room with its watercolor
                    of Versailles' gardens,
the blue Chinese hand-hooked rug—

following the hand-inked score,
                    listening hard with our hearts.

The music expands the room—
                    Juli bends toward us
the frail stem of her mortal
body. She watches our faces.
                    Her own face is unlined, shining

and beatific, as if
                    already, she has
been in the heavenly world.

Arguing Life for Life

arguing life for life even at your life's cost
—Muriel Rukeyser

Today in my office someone wanted to die
and I said *No*.

I leaned from the soft back of my chair
toward him as he bent forward, his back rounded
over his lap, his face in his huge hands.

I was long past menopause, family gone.
He didn't know this.

And I said: *No, because you can't do this*
to your children, and *No, because*
you won't always feel this way.
I told him how time is aloe to the burn.

He said he had a loaded rifle beneath his bed.
He said he could turn his wheel toward the roadside gully.

I said *No* to this man before me,
and I could feel an energy rise from somewhere
deep in my body and cast out beyond me,
toward him—a hot energy—a river, a rope.
It wanted to pull him up.

He closed against it. He shut up like a cave door
overgrown with tangled thorns.
He went somewhere else—
narrow passage, so dark and steep
I couldn't climb down.

I leaned back, let my hands fall;
both of us were tired of pain
and loss tallied week after week.

He didn't know how sometimes I stand
at my bedroom window looking out
where the white steeple lifts over the town,
wondering what is left to tether me to the earth.
We sat a long time in silence.

Small Wisdoms

Soon the blue myrtle will appear, as if from nowhere,
in the small woody patch at the back of the yard.
This blossoming means I've survived another winter.

I know what they meant now, those elders,
when they first said life is so short.
I mean I understand fully.

We are lit matches under the eye of the great fires,
a short flame, and that's all of it.

The stars continue as far as we know,
as far as we can see, and as far as we can't.

I am afraid. I mean I am scared to death
of all that can happen, and does,
in crowds, with guns, with the crazed mind
and the plain mean heart.

I fear the car out of control around the curve,
the sudden black wing-flash of chaos,
the new virus charging out of the jungle,

all those things you fear too,
though you may be better than I am at denial,
or maybe not.

A friend in her seventies has panic-attacks
since her husband's death. I'm on countdown
she says, as she packs lightly

for Greece and her lover, while I only hope,
after six weeks of dazzling sky and islands,
she'll return.

I am slipping on the scree on my mountain,
I am sliding, my knees give, my hips. If there
is a bottom to all this, I haven't found it.

If there are answers one comes to after a long life,
they are elusive,
the fly that takes off just after the swatter
is poised over it.

Pistachios

Take a simple thing like pistachios.
Think of them in their smooth brown cases
or cracked open to white meat shiny as a tooth.
Or think of them in ice cream, the green of mint
or spring or something more succulent,
an unnameable ecstasy.
Get into the nuttiness of them,
the unadorned goodness, then let the mind go
wherever it goes from there, to Romeo in the garden,
to the full brown nipples of Juliet. Let love
come into it
as the *raison d'etre* for all Being,
and because
someone's always starting a war, let war come into it,
though you wish it wouldn't.
Missiles over a ragged country;
worn-out people not turning back
to watch their homes on fire.
And from there go
to guns in the streets of our own country
and murders in the parks where no one is safe.
to feeble attempts—pistols
that can be fired only by their owners—
as if that would be enough to stop the killing.
Oh, but Romeo
in the garden, in blue, and the moon over.
Oh but Juliet on the balcony.
Oh but the strong vine
that can hold a man climbing.

And pistachio ice cream,
a green you could die for.
And pistachios themselves,
the simple nourishment,
the hard welcome apple,
the fallen fruit.

New Town

You are driving the U-Haul down Main St. on the way
to the second floor front apartment
in the old New Englander you are about to fill
with your four poster, sleeper sofa and misc. etc.
And you know, because you've seen the place once,
that it's dusty, musty, has a couple of curved walls
and a built-in spice cupboard in the kitchen
which was what sold you—character, that is—and
the tin porch roof like the one from your childhood
so you can already hear the security of rain on it.
But right now,
because you are seeing everything
with beginner's mind, you notice storefronts
whose interiors you might dimly imagine
if you thought to try—which you don't—and you notice
the citizens: hair the color of walnut stain,
gap-toothed men in pickups, college students lugging
book bags, five kids skateboarding a low wall, the whole town,
a conglomeration—and you figure that's okay, that's just fine,
because boredom is
one thing you've wanted to ditch.
Goodbye, goodbye to it. And goodbye to the highway
behind the old condo, its constant heavy metal racket;
goodbye to the job, its endless paper stacks.
This is "fleeing" pure and simple—
bent bar in the cage, new page, new rage for order,
new life blank
as what lies behind the walls of these buildings.
But nothing has happened yet,

(though from my vantage point here five years in your future)
I can promise you it will:
mice running kitchen counters, redneck absentee landlord,
yet another jackass boss, proof
you've flipped from the frying pan into the fire
just as they said you would.
But right now time's cranked
to a stop, you're driving the U-Haul down Main Street—
you've got your window open, sun heating your hair
and there is nothing but possibility.

Locked

Back from a flat-out day in New York, the museum,
the bus squeals into Hartford, drops us on a badly lit
dead-end at ten p.m., one block from the ghetto.

Some idiot has locked our cars behind the ten-foot
wrought iron fence and padlocked chain-linked gates.
We bang on the chains; no guard anywhere.

We call police; they don't come. We flag down
a fire truck. They say they've no right to break in
and don't do a damn thing for us.

Exhausted, thirsty, we lean against the fence
in the steaming city dark. From a tenement's second story,
a woman belts out an aria of pain:

Fuck you, you liar, you fucking asshole.
Above the cries of a child, above the raped-woman
howl of a siren, she belts it.

I know you're cheating. I can't take it.
I'm leaving.
Do you hear me? I'm leaving now.

We might be sitting in a theater where the picture's
gone dark, that's how bigger-than-life, almost mythic,
her voice is, pouring through the clouded night,

across backyards, across the universe.
She might be singing for all of us, so cold, so numb
in our own dead-end, wanting water, wanting to pee.

Then it stops. Restless as streetwalkers in the silence,
we pace up and down the fence. Blonde in black leather,
diminished, she wobbles on spikes out of haze.

Asks how come we're there—middle of nowhere.
We crowd around but she only laughs: *You think cops
will come. Ha! They never come.* And she staggers off.

Who knows what spurs on the guy then, in the wrinkled
blue suit who suddenly leaps—a condemned man's last lunge—
up ten feet of wrought iron, swings one leg over the top,

balances endless seconds above spikes and razor-wire,
before he flings the other over and jumps down
to our furious cheers. And who cares

by what right he rifles the cars for tools, and skilled
as a cat man, dismantles the lock—or by what right all of us,
lean our shoulders into the heavy gate, shove it back,

leap for our cars, and get the hell out of there.

Celebration

We anchored ourselves
against all warnings in the great
singular body of the crowd.

It was too late to decide otherwise,
too late to return to the TV's distance.
Night dropped its crystal ball from the ramparts

while above us, helicopters rattled the sky
and around us the crowd rocked,
sexual as fleas, loud as ambulances

and night's determined watchmen pressed through
keeping us safe, as though that were possible,
with their weapons and their thousand eyes.

What need to be among strangers
hurrahing for the new year drove us out
into this congregation, this clatter of pans?

Hope perhaps? Some need to persist in spite of?
Or simply our desire to touch shoulders
with the others, crazy as they are,

crazy as we are to believe in hope
at a time like this one. Crazy and necessary.
Meanwhile, the ball slides slowly earthward.

How the Dead Live

It is never a home—
it's a motel, an apartment, a rooming house,
a place to be where they don't own anything
and are transient as chess pieces.

There is seldom movement of the body itself,
and then only anonymous and drifting,
the wind through the headdress of a nun,
the wind through a sail luffing across a dark waste.

More often, the women are looking through
windows or doorways, are standing at bus-stops
on an empty street. They are waiting
and who can say for what.

The men stare deep into their coffee,
puzzle at their desks, the one lamp casting
a cruel white light on their faces—
austere and gray.

Sometimes the dead are naked, light folded
into each crease in their bodies so nothing
can be hidden. Many have bent postures
and eyes two-dimensional as thin slices of marbles.

They sit on curbstones for hours, their feet in gutters,
or smoke in brick corners
or push brooms down endless hallways
as if they have gone to utter decay—

as if there is no finger able to spin metal against flint,
no flame left at all, the cigarette lighter of the heart
gone out.

Late Love

What stomped your rooming-house rooms
was not peace, is not peace even now,
nor love quite.
                    Though there is that.

What is left: scraps of shredded beef
                              on the plate.

We have given in. Who will find us?

We are the last migratory birds
on the way to somewhere else.

We have outlived the thermometers.

Hospitals, list of doctors
as long as the envelope,
                    pills on the table.
I am tired of them.
I want to remember
the picnics of beginning.

I want to remember my promise
                    to hold on through.

Your worn reclining chair,
scattered magazines on the floor.

You watch me sleep
                    before I leave again.
Even in dream I can hear
the long freight clatter past
the boarded-up station.

Glosa after a Poem by Kelly Cherry

You were reading. I was dreaming
The color blue. The wind was hiding
In the trees and rain was streaming
Down the window, full of darkness.

The night outside was more than I
Had asked for. I wanted sleep
But sleep was an unfriendly stranger. The storm intended
To stay beyond its welcome. Once you looked up—
And for a moment I thought whatever it was
We'd lost would come colliding
Against whatever it is that still remains.
I almost thought we could begin again
Out of the storm—some tentative rare blossoming.
You were reading. I was dreaming.

Around us, the accoutrements of despair:
Faded chairs, a table piled with debts,
Our sick dog whimpering on the rug, dust
Descending everywhere, the thin quiet
That comes when love has moved past hope.
Only the nine-paned window dividing
Us from the outer storm—the blast of it.
Inside—the one-beat tock of the kitchen clock—
And even that seemed to be off kilter, sliding
Into *the color blue where the wind was hiding.*

What to do? Aging had overtaken us,
And ennui. I wanted to know the sparked breath

Of passion again, wanted to stand next
To someone, feeling the blood-blush rise
In my chest, the chemical rush like sap in the veins.
Is nothing meant to continue? Only this numbing
Left? I wanted to run—habit makes us prisoners.
Outside the room, wind clawed at the shingles,
The sap was running
In the trees—and rain was streaming.

You were reading. I was dreaming.
The dog was whimpering—your eyes
Were hiding. Beyond the window, the pines
Were dashing themselves against each other
In the rain. The lamp beside the chair was flickering.
You didn't move. I didn't express
Anything I was thinking. What good could it
Come to? There are things it's too late for.
I rose instead, let my fingers press
Down the window, full of darkness.

On Reaching Sixty-Five

We old women are close to wool sweaters.
When someone tries to tell us
what passes these days for the truth
we argue with them and refuse to believe.
Instead, we look to the stars for faith and confusion.
Where both are ample.

I hold the door open
and look down the snowbound road.
See how the stranger appears on it,
gradually and from a great distance.
If he comes close enough,
I will allow him to enter, or perhaps not,
given the certainty of loss.

Once there was a man full of appreciation
for his own mind.
I tried to enter him and failed.
His suitcases bumped together as he left.

Sometimes I wonder how I came to this place.
Life, like a smoke ring, lifts
into the old air
where I can't put my finger on it.

But something indefinable and fragile remains
of the orchard, the way it was at the peak of harvest—
sweet and humming.

three/

Duties of the Spirit

one of the duties of the spirit is joy, and another is serenity...
                    −Thorton Wilder in a letter to Paul Stephenson, 1930

If the first is joy—
the rhumba at sunrise,
a three-note whistle in the sugar maple—

and the second is serenity—
a chair by a quiet window,
the wind fading down the hill at sleep—

then the third must be grief—
rock-tight, then loosening like scarves the wind takes
across the ocean while on the shore
the shells' empty houses lie scattered.

And if the first is in the brief seconds
which are all we can keep of happiness

and if the second waits alone in the hour
where the pond smoothes out, its surface
unbroken and the moon in it—

then the third which is grief comes again and again
longer and more than we wanted
or ever wished for

to wash us clean with its saltwater,
to empty our throats, and fill them
again with bloodroot song,

And if the first
duty of the spirit is leaping joy,
and the second,
the slow stroll of serenity,

then grief, the third, comes bending on his walking stick,
holding a trowel to dig where the loves have gone,

and he weighs down your shoulders, ties a rawhide necklace
hung with a stone around your neck, and hangs on and on.
But the first is slippery joy.

Desire #1

Wanting everything to come together:
the horses that run by the dark river
the cliffs where birds nest
and rise more freely than ghosts
other callings in the low grasses
wings and fortunes
the nest the pigeons made in the loft.
There is a place
wrapped in silver
where the elephant raises its trunk
and the crocodiles
open the leather pouches of their lids.
Fear and caution—
we accept our fate.
Fences knocked over
are always blind.
If sleep continued all day
there would be no language
to erase the last of darkness.
Against another hand
you scrape your fingers to bone.
A singular truth is sung loudly
as if with a megaphone.
Desire is one condition of the soul.
Our bones move us forward,
we grab whatever we can.

Desire #2

It struggles like a salmon thrashing
upstream brave on the journey that finishes
in quiet circling—roe drifting down in clouds
beneath riverwater—little globes of continuance,

or it pedals hot as a racer in red trunks,
along a course that climbs and descends
seven local hills, heads out into the wild
and back again in all extremities of weather.

It is nothing like the chill paten of the moon,
nor the hot pallet of the sun sprawled
like Magdalene on the bed of sky—but something
in-between—a gentle beast with nostrils flared.

It creeps forward from the wiry thicket
to catch you from behind,
paws clapped over your eyes:
Guess who. Guess who.

Or it slides slippery as the striped whipsnake
that streaks through the western grasslands—
flash of tongue, glitter of eye—
gone too soon.

Desire #3

These days, no matter how she wills it
to be different, sadness presses like storm clouds
on her body and even the sun
is a hot boy who turns away from her.

It has something to do with money, that knife
in the chest of not having it, or the portion of it
that could buy a white house with black shutters
plus a ticket on a tramp steamer to everywhere.

Even more to do with space,
not having enough in the two room containment—
the apartment she lives in which is not
and never will be a home.

And it has plenty to do with recognition,
the clapping of hundreds of hands, her moment
alone on a grand stage, or even to be first
in the life of one other.

She understands it should suffice to rise,
even achingly, alive from the mattress each morning.
She ought to kneel on rice for hours in gratitude—
to be shouting praise for the paw of the cat

on her cheek, for the maintenance man
with his plunger and plow, for the host
of white-throated sparrows, their Old Sam Peabody
songs from the woodlot, for the up-reaching

maples, their breeze-released voices, for her grandson
in another state beginning to name the world
two words at a time, for everything
that starts again or is new again, or persists.

But how often she does give praise, if not to a god,
then at least to light, its thousand permutations,
to herons performing tai chi in a salt marsh,
to the unbroken sea and the broken slipper shells.

How hard she tries to be good, to be good enough.
And fails. More often, she feels like the man
in the novel about Africa, who stumbles like a child
through the rain forest howling: *I want, I want, I want.*

Brief Encounter

How easily we slid through waters too slick
with swirls of reflected light
to give back our faces,

under *Il Ponte del Diavolo,* The Bridge of Sighs,
into a canal that ended in a circular pool,
quays rising like walls.

One jubilant hour of gondolier music,
the tenor voice, the accordion: *Angela Mia,*
Luna Rossa, and above us

shutters slamming across a window.
Two small mongrels yapping.
All time was with us

in that circumscribed world.
Now, I wonder if you even remember me.
Still, this mattered, this brief touching,

the way someone slides out of mist
and into mist, whatever was
to whatever is.

We turned in that moment to face the night,
the captured sea, our hair night-dampened,
the magic we hauled in like full nets.

Later, we linked arms and strolled
along the Via Triestina
to the nearly empty Casino di Venezia.

Easy, that night, to trust fate.
Easy to believe there is no parting,
that nothing could bring us down.

Old Woman Dreams

He came to her finally in his torn jeans and soft
tan jacket, came from feeding the horses,
their sweat still on his palms,
came redolent of hay, honey from his hives—
Solomon's Song on his lips.
Came with the old scar on his cheek where
she left the chaste imprint of a kiss.
Younger, impossibly younger,
he told her what she wanted to hear.
But only in dream, night, the color of his black hair.

Around him, her arms wound like his branches,
his eyes were a garden she ached to lie down in.
They met in a wind-rush, and what she remembers
is a craving to follow where he was leading.
Also the impression of dissolving
against the astonishment of his chest.
Her desire seems to have its own life and will not be
expelled no matter how often she tries to banish it.

Somehow an old woman feels all this. Is it so odd?
She's heard a dream embodies a message
from the totem spirit, like the fox
who emerges in flame from the forests
and goes to hide in the morning hours.

The Winter House

It is always minus zero
      meaning the absence of light
            and an ice that slicks all surfaces.

Behind closed doors and drapes,
      the windows give back nothing,
            air's an entropy of dust.

Whoever lives there—
      lives alone,
            intent on doing what comes

most easily, eating what can be
      simply taken—or not at all,
            curling themselves into an absence

as though the only world exists
      beyond plate glass—
            and is unreachable,

the future, a room within a room
      within a room, Chinese boxes,
            each smaller than the last.

Beneath the roof—its freight
      of snow and sadness,
            what they want is nothing more

than the welcome body of sleep
descending
over their own body

like a lover who arrives
with a flower in the night—
and will not be sent away.

The Room

The clock pressed the hours by,
frost blinded the windows.
The language beyond them disappeared
into ice.
If you sit in such a room you can forget.
The orange cat stretched out full-length
on the table and slept
the sleep of a careless one.
I lived there—or did not live—
the future a cutoff thing,
the past not part of me anymore—
smoke flying back from the train
on a Russian steppe
in an old complicated novel.
Gone, gone. Gone, gone. And goodbye.
In that standstill time, the cat and I
studied each other like mirrors—
his topaz inscrutable eyes.
I thought I was safe in the room.
The plow came to plow through the whiteness.
Because I was locked in my body
the frost climbed higher.
Because I was not safe
my arms wrapped around me.
One minute became the next—
nothing shifted
except the cat
who jumped down and went to his bowl.
In the bookcase, the books leaned

to the right and glazed over.
The white Greek rugs and three bright watercolors
dulled to the gray of a wolf's pelt.
The ice entered and shook the curtains.
Then it was time to move, however slightly,

some action to break the frozen surface.
Still I did not move but the cat disappeared
into his hiding place between the boxes
under the bed.
I think of the people out in the world
moving around in their lives.
in/out, up/down, bending, standing,
wheels under them, the open skies.
How brave they all are.
In that room, I held fear
like the egg of a beast, about to break open.

Applewood, the End of October

Anna, in her blue sweater, with her broom,
sweeps the walk again, a useless task since the wind
will paste it with more leaves.

And although the sky fills with the yellow fans
of the ginkgo tree, and sunlight clear as a Waterford decanter,
in the apartment across the way, Sarah's lamp

glows in her window as if, at ninety-three, she is trying
to ward off the darkness that comes
from a two room place with only three windows—

as I am, here, with my own lamps, in my identical rooms.
I know this is my last place: from a home, to a condo,
to the light-filled apartment on Beaver Street,

to here—each move a divestiture, each blouse
and skirt assessed, most of them bagged for Goodwill,
unneeded dishes smashed in a barrel, the albums

bestowed to the kids at Christmas. What is left is
what I can't bear to leave behind. Even then, books
overwhelm bookshelves, clothes cram the one closet.

I sit in the window, writing on graph paper, resting
the Rhodia pad on Rusty Cat's window ledge.
He jumps up, extends tentative claws toward my arm,

then butts it instead with his soft forehead and leaps
to the floor again. He is being gracious; I am
trespasser here, this is his watching spot, not mine.

On the patio, the geranium lets go of its last blossoms
and nothing is left of the basil in the clay pot but stalks.
Soon, Anna will die and Sarah also.

Almost weekly, the ambulance races in
to the spot reserved for it.
Someone is taken away.

Because death is so close and coming on

Because death is coming closer with each spring, and the springs
follow one on the other like a procession of celebrants
for whom ritual is everything,
I want to hold out my hand to each one, begging them
to stop, but they keep on walking in their crimson robes
      and three-cornered hats
        as the trees break into flower above their heads.

          *

Because death is near, I want to gather my various past lives
into baskets of reeds with sturdy handles; I want especially
to gather the loves, and even the days
where nothing much was happening except for the way
images were taking shape, forming reality and undoing it again.

          *

Meaning eludes me and then it doesn't
                     and then it does.
Hide and seek around the lilac bushes.
What weaves a whole life together? Makes it cohere?
Memory is a poor weaver with flimsy thread.

          *

Death is coming and what will I be after? And can I
bear to leave the earth which I have always loved—
even in the absence of light that is depression.

Now, in late April, the willow turns to the gold that trumpets
spring into being. The flush over the hills comes again and again
each end of April with the same predictability as April itself comes.

*

Because death comes—there will be a season when I
will not be here to notice. Because death comes,
there will be short days of flowers on my gravestone
and eons when no one remembers my name.

*

There are days left yet, less full perhaps, than the days before them,
ordinary perhaps, more surrounded by walls,
but also the existence of laughter which persists like a miracle.

Pain

Called from the willow trees where I could not
   see it—and those weeds that had blackened,
      voiceless in the frost.

Came nearer, like the emergency lantern
   a bent man carries—violet, then red,
      then violet again.

Entered here through the wound in my left side
   and no rest—
      no way to understand

where or why the foxes
   who have always sustained me
      have hidden.

I pull up a comforter
   though I haven't cleared
      the ache away.

There is no way to explain
   how it rises to the throat—
      how it takes its life

from what it touched before
   of the sun—
      old burning tiger.

Complaining doesn't help—
    those I need spinning away from me,
        like music hall dancers.

Fire climbs my chest, my shoulders, my side,
    or gnaws, or coils there and unbraids
        and unbraids—hissing until I am quiet.

Couplets by the Cove after a Hard Year

On a flat rock I sit sketching a pinkweed. An aphid,
transparent, climbs down to trespass across the page.

One duck floats on the white sails of her wings
across light too sharp for my eyes.

A naked toddler wades ankle deep, his mother
ready to pluck him up.

Rank odor rises from the marsh.
Two more golden insects escape the weed's stem

and wander the page's white landscape
as I draw their miniature bodies.

Below my rock, the water laps in—gentle as hands
on a breast—bits of foam, blades of sunlight.

Dried leaves, blood brown, mend the fractures
between the boulders. Waves' gravely speech.

There is healing here: poultice of salt, bandage of moss,
the little enduring hips of the beach roses.

"The Point of Deepest Loveliness"

after David Brendan Hopes

Where was it—loveliness? My daughter's birth,
her seven pound body, blood-smeared, grasped upside down
in light intense enough to blur the edges between us.

Was it as far as Florence—three children peering
through a balcony's iron grate
or as near home as family at a holiday table?

Was it light through stained glass in a still church
or common as a kitchen,
or a Sunday afternoon, room dimmed

by drawn shades, when a man opened
my legs and lifted them
over his shoulders?

I grasp the fullness in the fullness of days,
in the surplus of filling, my body blooms,
the moments explode:

Lake Memphremagog, sunset brushed
the satin surface orange and bronze,
childhood, our rowboat

small in the middle of the lake,
beneath us pickerel, and perch,
the lake weeds tangling around our oars.

I write about beauty; I cannot resist.
What else redeems suffering?
Any god is a jester.

This afternoon I watched a line of relatives
parade past my window. They were clearing out
the apartment of the woman who died.

A pole lamp went by, four curved chairs,
curtains, sheets, a comforter, a ficus tree.
They bent under the weight.

They pressed forward. But deepest loveliness—
deep sable silk of my dog sleeping,
quiet of the room shivering in candlelight,

and in memory: a flat water and nine blue herons rising
from a rookery in the dead spars of hemlocks,
while at pond-edge, I watched from the blind.

First Born

we are made of stars —Carl Sagan

In the shadow of the new crib, my daughter-in-law
sleeps on her side, curled like protection
around her own expanded belly,
holding the child, even now,
before its birth, in her arms.

Child and mother both sleep
                     in a kind of waiting.

It is almost time: In the nebula
of her womb, dust gathers—millions, billions
of cells, a cosmic cloud.
               Soon
the first pain, slow, imperceptible,
will radiate across Lynn's lower back,
then her abdomen,
increasing over the hours—

pain after pain—accelerating to violence—
the child's body assaulting
her body, and she wanting it, calling it on.
                This
is how a new star gets born: the wreckage
of rip and tear, collision and thrust, the inexorable
gravity pushing down, all in a rush—
an explosion of light.

              But for now
in the cosmic quiet
   of this night, my daughter-in-law sleeps.

On the Roundness of Everything: An August Nocturne

At midnight
              in the cooled air
                            there was the moon.

And before that, in the hot day, many were the moons of zinnias.

And the whole time there was the moon of my thoughts in its skull basket.

One was the color vermillion
              and others the red and yellow of celebration.

One swallows the universe
              like snow swallows a field.

Months from now when the snow moon gambols the sky like a white rabbit
                    in white snow.

I'll chop rutabaga and beets for the soup; buy heavy cream.

Now, a breast pours its liquid
                    into an infant's mouth in the next state.

The amorphous shadows under the maples are
                  where we lie down together.

Remaking "*Les Deux Mulets*"

after Chagall

I have cut away the bandit with the knife in his teeth
and now I can pretend the red on the chest of the mule
is not blood but blossom. I have cut away the bags of grain
that were lying on the mule's back, making of themselves a burden.
I have buried them behind the night. And now I can pretend
the second mule is only sleeping; I can pretend the night
pulses with dreaming, imagine extravagant music.
This is how I want to handle the trouble
in the world: fracture the sky into floating triangles, give it
not one moon but two, mount the changed earth
against a yellow background,
turn all the murders into sleeping peaceful bodies.

Request

I'm asking for the clarity
of a fogged-in morning,
its half-illumination of trees
& a world that shimmers
slightly out of reach.
I'm asking for the cranking
geese make overhead
to turn into words I can,
for once, understand,
& for the insects at the back door
in the evening to touch me
with their delicate antennae.
Moreover, I'm asking that
the troubles of the earth withdraw,
that the fires stop being hungry,
that the hatred stops being,
that the stars rock gently, gently,
in their great sockets.
Moreover
I'm wanting (o god)
plum purples, scarlets,
blues. I'm wanting a surplus
of symphony, the overfall, overfull
of water down rocks,
a nest of cinnamon & the sweet dolor
of leaves burning.
I'm wanting to come so close
to a man that I inhale his breath,
that my fingers map his skin,

touch skin again.
Too long untouching, untouched.
I'm asking for whatever it is
that makes my heart light
& drift down featherwise
& settle like pillows.
I'm asking if it's possible—
if it's still possible.

The Composer Says This Is How We Should Live Our Lives

He lifts his violin and gives us the fox
in Ireland running with wild abandon
along the cliff-edge above the wild Irish Sea

and I am back in Connemara where even
the pasture stones have names and the green
slopes are plentiful with stones and the sea-wind

where there are no trees to stop it rollicks
across the commonage and the sea's a wild rolling
and the composer's brown hair is whipping around

his young intense face as his arm jigs and swings
the bow across the strings and his body is swaying
and his shoulders are leaping and the music is leaping

and the fox is running with such joy along that cliff
red fox brilliant green pasture cerulean sky
and the wind and the white-capped

plum-blue ocean and a man's foot measuring time
in the sun that is beyond brilliant and the fox is leaping
forward along the cliff-edge.

The Leave-Taking

I wanted to be serene, without companions, rocking
      in the wooden garden swing,
 only my own desires to answer,

no one who would go away from me,
      no one hanging up the telephone,
no one passing their fiery torch along my life.

When you walked out from the birch shadows
      where I had not seen you hiding,
and the flowers surrounded us, the mockingbirds

welcomed you with their multifarious voices,
      but you chose
to become one of them, taking leave from the hedges,

your wings broadening in flight, then disappearing
      over the fields beyond the gate.
I swept up dropped petals and held them

in the cup of my two palms, absorbing their velvet,
      their edgy fragrance,
before I uncurled my fingers, and let them fall.

Acknowledgments

Comstock Review: "When Women Went Downtown"

Crab Orchard Review: "Poem for a Composer at Eighty-Three"

Chile Verde: "Arguing Life for Life"

Crying Sky: "Request"; "Celebration"

Diner: "Quotitian Poem"; "Desire"

Larcom Review: "Evidence"; "Glosa after a Poem by Kelly Cherry"; "The Composer Says This Is How We Should Live Our Lives"

Malahat Review: "How the Dead Live"

Margie: "Because death is so close and coming on"

Mid-American Review: "Duties of the Spirit"

Nimrod: "Talking to Myself in This Late Year"; "Pistachios"

North American Review: "Answers for the Scientists Who Have Wired the Heads of Zebra Finches to Study Their Dreams"

Rattle: "Fun"

Passages North: "Late Love"

Poetry Northwest: "Locked"

Praire Schooner: "When Too Much Has Happened"

The following poems first appeared in chapbooks:

Lives of Others: "Arguing Life for Life"; *Small Songs of Pain:* "Remaking *Les Deux Mulets*"

The first four lines of "Glosa After a Poem by Kelly Cherry" are from Kelly Cherry's poem "Reading, Dreaming, Hiding" in *God's Loud Hand,* Louisiana State University Press, 1993, and are reprinted with permission of the press.

The epigraph to "Duties of the Spirit" by Thornton Wilder was copied from a letter framed on the wall of the Dorset Colony House in Dorset, VT.

I am grateful for the phrase "the point of deepest loveliness" (from my poem of that name), which was taken from a post by David Hopes to the Crewrt listserv (with his permission).

Many thanks to my friends, students and workshop members who've been so supportive to me in my development as a poet, and to all those who've made suggestions on these poems both individually and in manuscript. Especially to Susan Roney-O'Brien, Laura Kennelly, Jean Tupper, Gina Tabasso, Ilya Kaminsky and Carlos Martinez who generously read drafts of the manuscript and offered many helpful suggestions, and to Herb Yood, my good friend and sounding-board. Thanks also to Gray Jacobik and Jane Meneghini for their help with proofreading; to the Macdowell Colony where some of these poems were written.

Much gratitude to Brendan Galvin for his encouragement through many years, to my family who sustain me, and to Donald Sheehan of The Frost Place, whose deeply spiritual life and love of poetry are a constant inspiration.

And, above all, thanks to Mary Oliver, whose way of living is my benchmark and whose continuing belief in me is what keeps me going through the days when I am in doubt and darkness.